AL

THE EASY KEYBOARD LIBRARY

BIG COLLECTION

Volume Three

Music arranged and processed by Barnes Music Engraving Ltd
East Sussex TN22 4HA, England

Production by Sadie Cook

Cover design by xheight design limited

Reproduced and printed by Halstan & Co. Ltd., Amersham, Bucks., England

Published 1999

786.92 BIG

10.99

Abide With Me

Words by Henry Francis Lyte / Music by Will Henry Monk

Suggested Registration: Flute
Rhythm: Soft Rock
Tempo: ♩ = 88

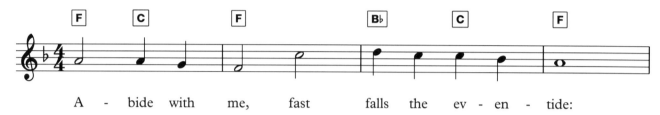

A - bide with me, fast falls the ev - en - tide:

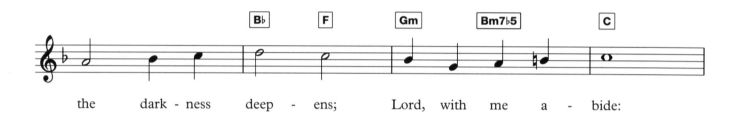

the dark - ness deep - ens; Lord, with me a - bide:

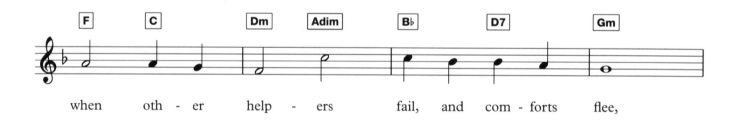

when oth - er help - ers fail, and com - forts flee,

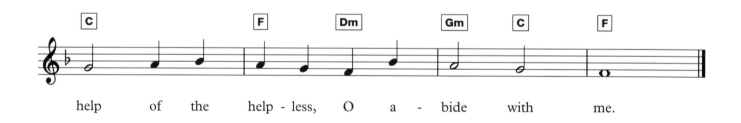

help of the help - less, O a - bide with me.

1   Abide with me, fast falls the eventide:
    the darkness deepens; Lord, with me abide:
    when other helpers fail, and comforts flee,
    help of the helpless, O abide with me.

2   Swift to its close ebbs out life's little day;
    earth's joys grow dim, its glories pass away;
    change and decay in all around I see:
    O thou who changest not, abide with me.

3   I need thy presence every passing hour;
    what but thy grace can foil the tempter's power?
    who like thyself my guide and stay can be?
    through cloud and sunshine, Lord, abide with me.

4   Hold thou thy cross before my closing eyes:
    shine through the gloom, and point me to the skies:
    heaven's morning breaks, and earth's vain shadows flee;
    in life, in death, O Lord, abide with me.

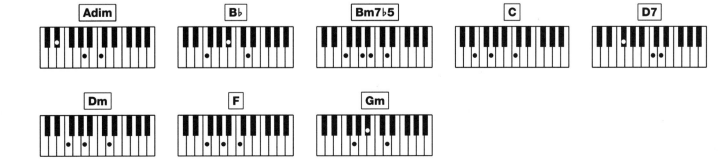

Almost Like Being In Love

Words by Alan Jay Lerner / Music by Frederick Loewe

Suggested Registration: Jazz Guitar
Rhythm: Swing
Tempo: ♩ = 132

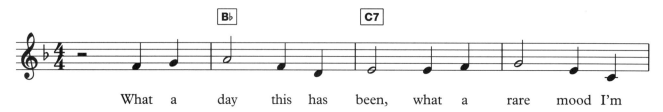

What a day this has been, what a rare mood I'm

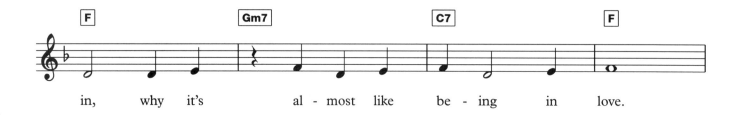

in, why it's al - most like be - ing in love.

There's a smile on my face for the whole hu - man

race, why it's al - most like be - ing in love.

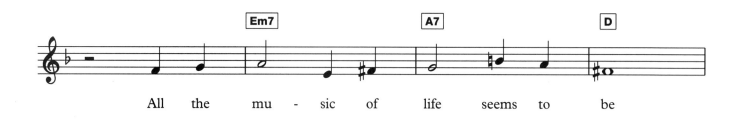

All the mu - sic of life seems to be

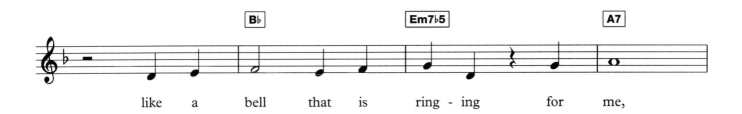

like a bell that is ring - ing for me,

and from the way that I feel, when that bell starts to

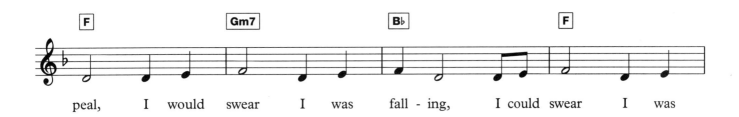

peal, I would swear I was fall - ing, I could swear I was

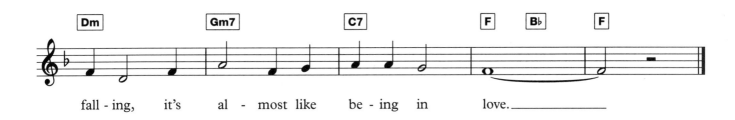

fall - ing, it's al - most like be - ing in love._____

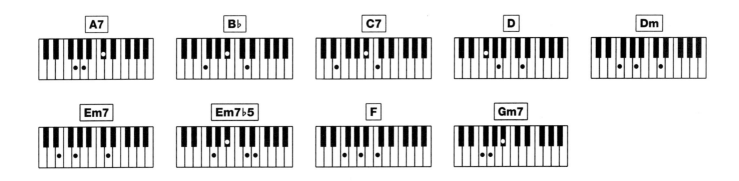

Baby Love

Words and Music by Brian Holland, Eddie Holland and Lamont Dozier

Suggested Registration: Electric Piano
Rhythm: Shuffle
Tempo: ♩ = 130

Bright Eyes

Words and Music by Mike Batt

Suggested Registration: Electric Piano
Rhythm: Soft Rock
Tempo: ♩ = 104

Is it a kind of__ dream,__ float - ing out on the

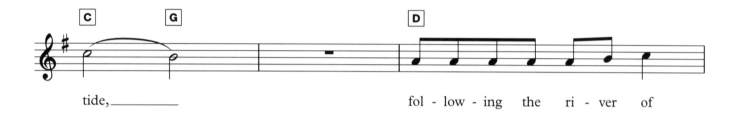

tide,_____ fol - low - ing the ri - ver of

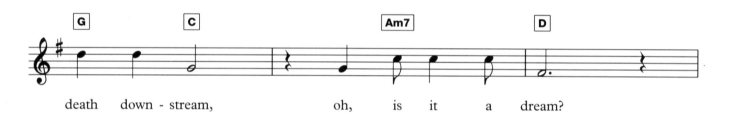

death down - stream, oh, is it a dream?

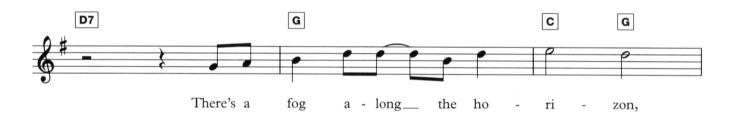

There's a fog a - long__ the ho - ri - zon,

a strange glow in the sky,_____ and

no - bo - dy seems__ to know where you go,

But Not For Me

Music and Lyrics by George Gershwin and Ira Gershwin

Suggested Registration: Vibraphone
Rhythm: Swing
Tempo: ♩ = 130

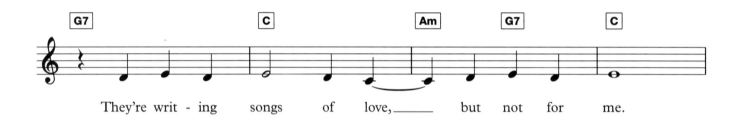

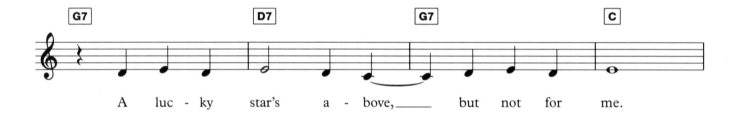

They're writ - ing songs of love,____ but not for me.

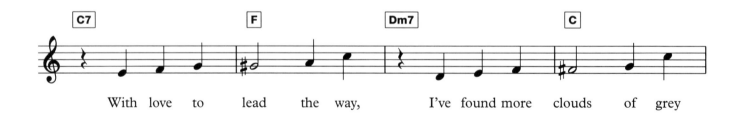

A luc - ky star's a - bove,____ but not for me.

With love to lead the way, I've found more clouds of grey

than a - ny Rus - sian play could guar - an - tee.

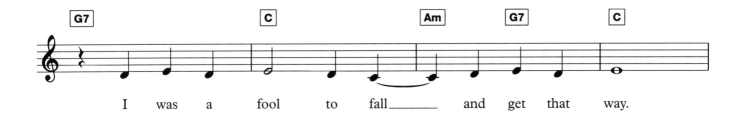

I was a fool to fall___ and get that way.

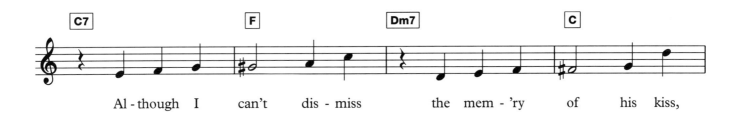

Heigh - ho! A - las! and al - so lack - a - day!

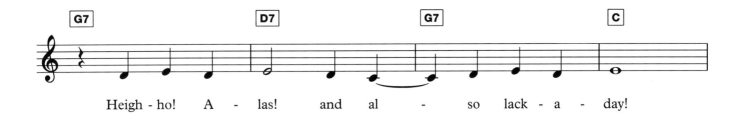

Al - though I can't dis - miss the mem - 'ry of his kiss,

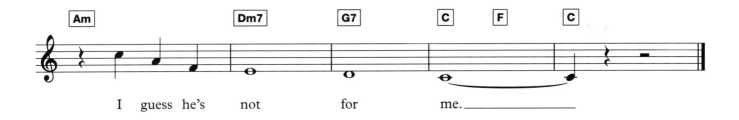

I guess he's not for me.___

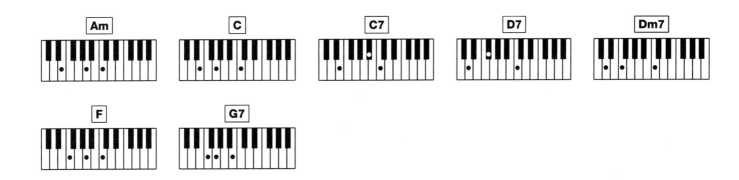

Cavatina

By Stanley Myers

Suggested Registration: Strings
Rhythm: Pop Waltz
Tempo: ♩ = 100

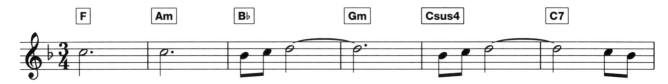

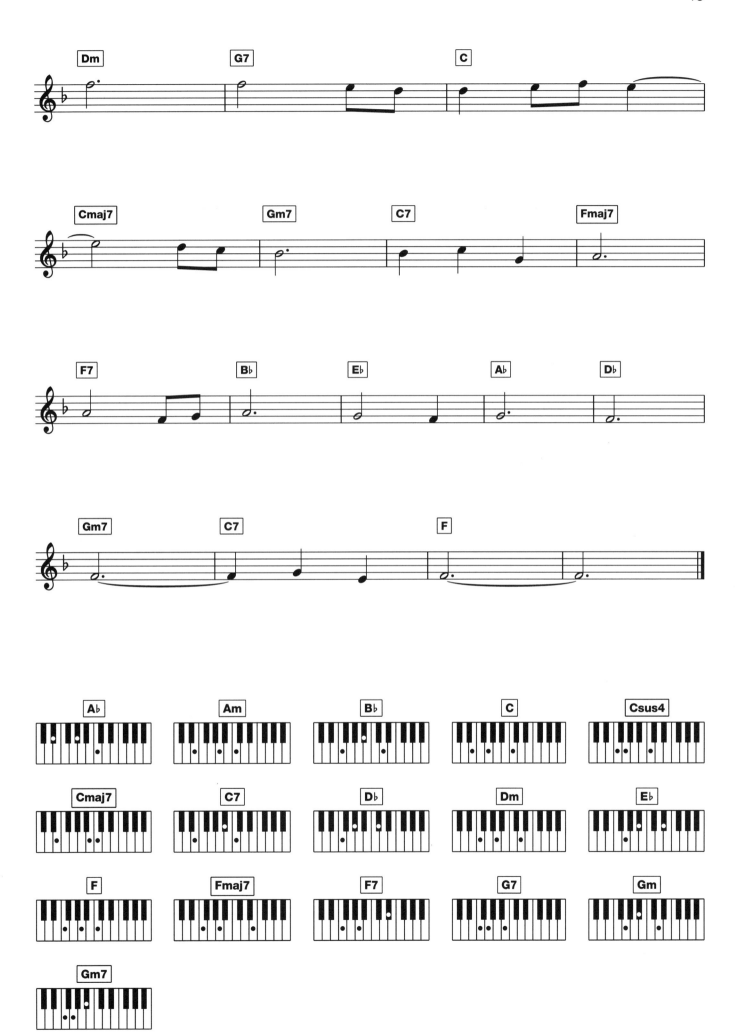

Congratulations

Words and Music by Bill Martin and Phil Coulter

Suggested Registration: Clarinet
Rhythm: Swing
Tempo: ♩ = 180

Day By Day

Words and Music by Stephen Schwartz

Suggested Registration: Flute
Rhythm: Rock / 8 Beat
Tempo: ♩ = 132

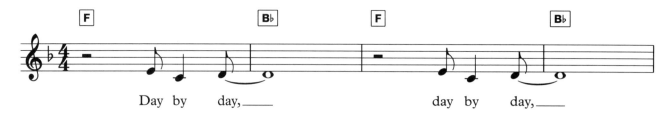

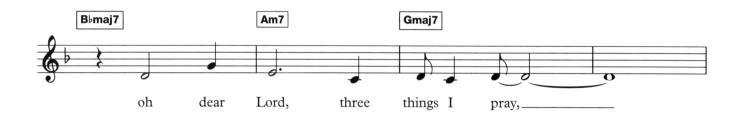

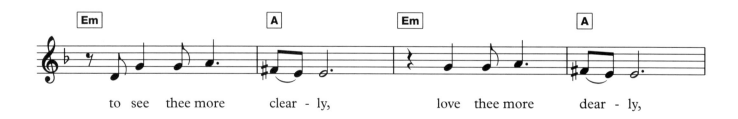

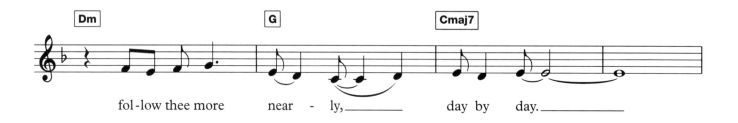

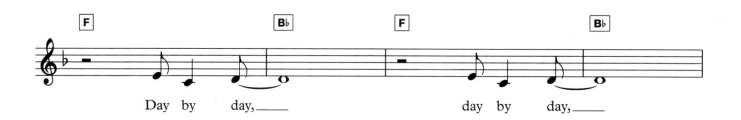

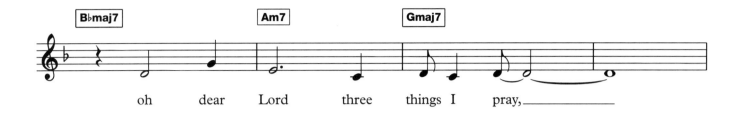

oh dear Lord three things I pray,___

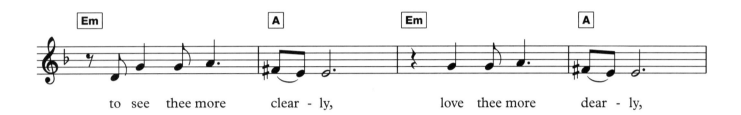

to see thee more clear - ly, love thee more dear - ly,

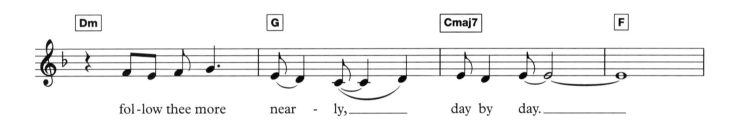

fol-low thee more near - ly,___ day by day.___

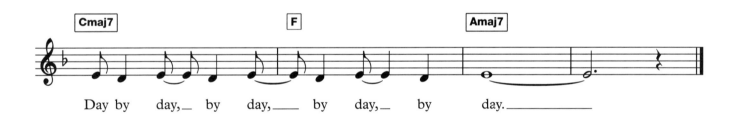

Day by day,_ by day,___ by day,_ by day.___

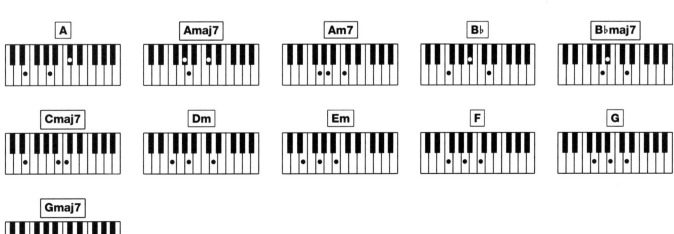

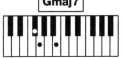

DECK THE HALL WITH BOUGHS OF HOLLY

Welsh traditional

Suggested Registration: Piano
Rhythm: Country Rock
Tempo: ♩ = 80

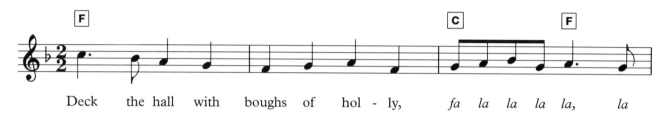

Deck the hall with boughs of hol - ly, *fa la la la la, la*

la la la. 'Tis the sea - son to be jol - ly,

fa la la la la, la la la la. Don we now our

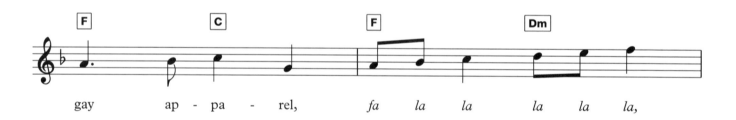

gay ap - pa - rel, *fa la la la la la,*

la la la. Troll the an - cient yule - tide ca - rol,

fa la la la la, la la la la.

1 Deck the hall with boughs of holly,
   Fa la la la la, la la la la.
   'Tis the season to be jolly,
   Fa la la la la, la la la la.
   Don we now our gay apparel,
   Fa la la, la la la, la la la.
   Troll the ancient yuletide carol,
   Fa la la la la, la la la la.

2 See the blazing yule before us,
   Fa la la la la, la la la la.
   Strike the harp and join the chorus,
   Fa la la la la, la la la la.
   Follow me in merry measure,
   Fa la la, la la la, la la la.
   While I tell of yuletide treasure,
   Fa la la la la, la la la la.

3 Far away the old year passes,
   Fa la la la la, la la la la.
   Hail the new, ye lads and lasses,
   Fa la la la la, la la la la.
   Sing we joyous all together,
   Fa la la, la la la, la la la.
   Heedless of the wind and weather,
   Fa la la la la, la la la la.

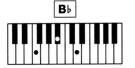
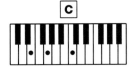
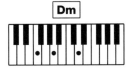
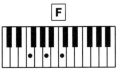

Dream Lover

Words and Music by Bobby Darin

Suggested Registration: Saxophone
Rhythm: 8 Beat
Tempo: ♩ = 132

Ev - ery night   I   hope and   pray_____   a dream lov - er will

come my   way,   a girl to hold   in my   arms,_____   and know the ma - gic

of her   charms, be-cause I   want   a   girl   to call___   my

own,___   I want a   dream lov-er, so   I don't have to dream a - lone._____

—   Some day, I   don't know how,_____   I hope you'll

EMBRACEABLE YOU

Music and Lyrics by George Gershwin and Ira Gershwin

Suggested Registration: Piano
Rhythm: Swing
Tempo: ♩ = 104

Em - brace me   my sweet, em - brace - a - ble   you._____

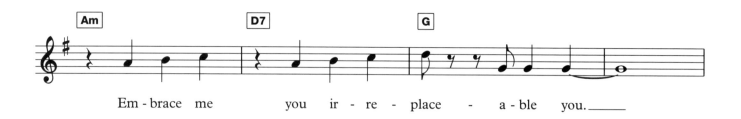

Em - brace me   you ir - re - place - a - ble   you._____

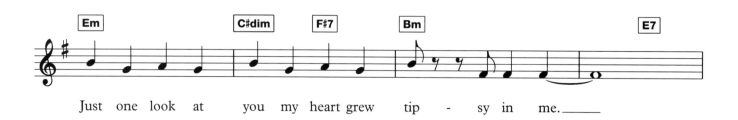

Just one look at   you my heart grew   tip - sy in   me._____

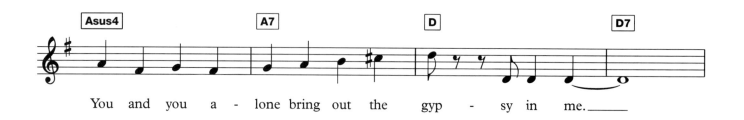

You and you a - lone bring out the   gyp - sy in   me._____

I love all the ma-ny charms a-bout you.____

A-bove all I want my arms a-bout you.____

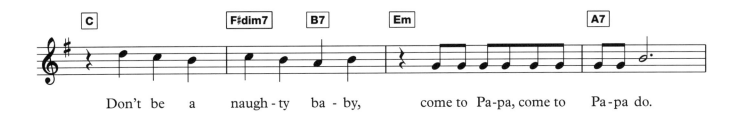

Don't be a naugh-ty ba-by, come to Pa-pa, come to Pa-pa do.

My sweet em-brace - a-ble you.____

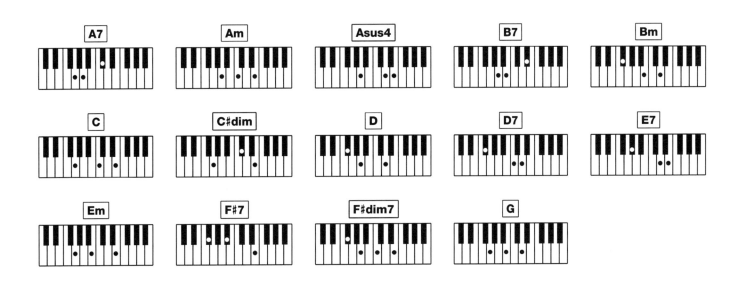

ENDLESS LOVE

Words and Music by Lionel Richie

Suggested Registration: Acoustic Guitar
Rhythm: Soft Rock
Tempo: ♩ = 92

My love, ___ there's on - ly you in my life,

the on - ly thing that's right. ___ My

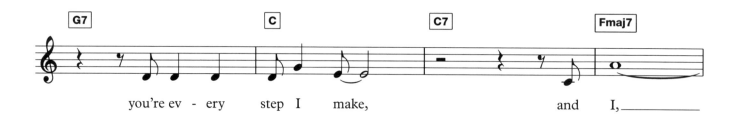

first ___ love, you're ev - ery breath that I take,

you're ev - ery step I make, and I, ___

___ I want to share all my love ___ with ___ you, ___

© 1971 & 1994 Brockman Music, PGP Music and Intersong USA Inc, USA
Warner/Chappell Music Ltd, London W6 8BS

Für Elise

By Ludwig Van Beethoven

Suggested Registration: Piano
Rhythm: Waltz
Tempo: ♩ = 104

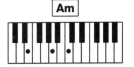

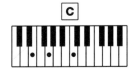

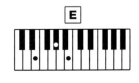

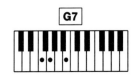

GET HERE

Words and Music by Brenda Russell

Suggested Registration: Piano
Rhythm: Ballad
Tempo: ♩ = 54

GREENSLEEVES

Traditional

Suggested Registration: Oboe
Rhythm: Waltz
Tempo: ♩ = 116

A - las my

love,___ you do me wrong___ to cast me out___ dis -

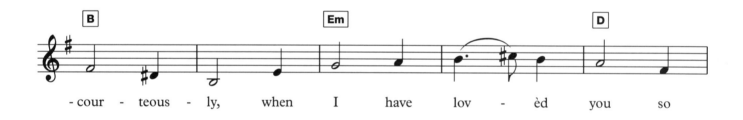

- cour - teous - ly, when I have lov - èd you so

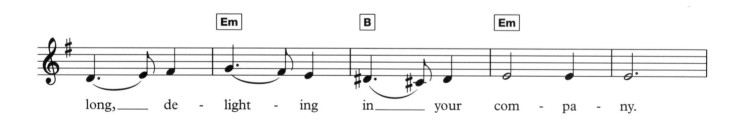

long,___ de - light - ing in___ your com - pa - ny.

Green - sleeves___ was my de - light,___ oh, Green -

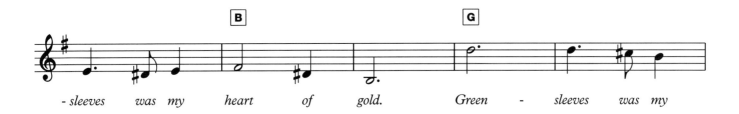

-sleeves   was   my   heart   of   gold.   Green   -   sleeves   was   my

la   -   dy   love,___   and   who   but   my   la   -   dy   Green   -   sleeves.

1   Alas my love, you do me wrong
    To cast me out discourteously,
    When I have lovèd you so long,
    Delighting in your company.
        Greensleeves was my delight,
        Oh, Greensleeves was my heart of gold.
        Greensleeves was my lady love,
        And who but my lady Greensleeves.

2   I have been ready at your hand,
    To grant whatever you would crave.
    I have both wagered life and land,
    Your love and good will for to have.
        Greensleeves . . .

3   I bought thee kerchiefs to thy head
    That were wrought fine, and gallantly.
    I kept thee both at board and bed,
    Which cost my purse well favouredly.
        Greensleeves . . .

4   Thy smock of gold so crimson red,
    With pearls bedecked sumptously,
    The like no other lasses had,
    And yet thou wouldest not love me.
        Greensleeves . . .

5   Thy gown was of the grassy green,
    Thy sleeves of satin hanging by,
    Which made thee be our harvest queen,
    And yet thou wouldest not love me.
        Greensleeves . . .

6   Thou couldst desire no earthly thing,
    But still thou hadst it readily.
    Thy music still to play and sing,
    And yet thou wouldest not love me.
        Greensleeves . . .

7   Well, I will pray to God on high,
    That thou my constancy mayst see,
    And that yet once before I die,
    Thou will vouchsafe to love me.
        Greensleeves . . .

8   Greensleeeves, now farewell, adieu!
    God I pray to prosper thee,
    For I am still thy lover true,
    Come once again and love me.
        Greensleeves . . .

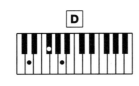
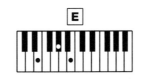
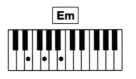

A Groovy Kind Of Love

Words and Music by Toni Wine and Carole Bayer Sager

Suggested Registration: Acoustic Guitar
Rhythm: Pop 8 Beat
Tempo: ♩ = 86

When I'm feel-ing blue, all I have to do is take a look at

you, then I'm not so blue. When you're close to me, I can feel your

heart beat, I can hear you breath-ing in my ear. Would-n't you a-

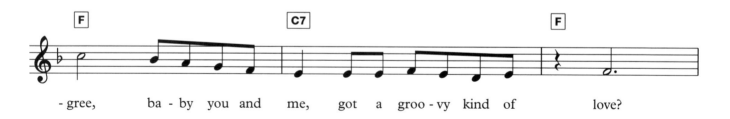

-gree, ba-by you and me, got a groo-vy kind of love?

We've got a groo-vy kind of love. A-ny time you want to, you can turn me

on to a-ny-thing you want to, a-ny time at all. When I taste your

lips, oh I start to shi - ver, can't con-trol the qui - ver - ing in -

- side. Would-n't you a - gree, ba - by you and me got a groo-vy kind of

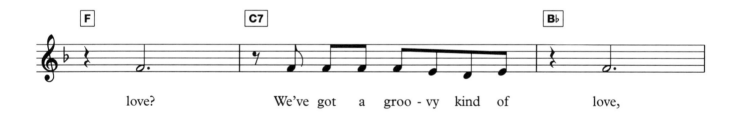

love? We've got a groo-vy kind of love,

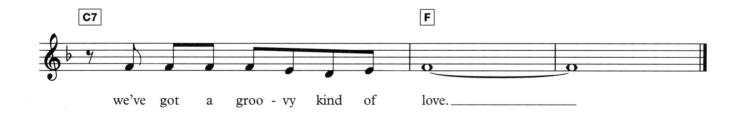

we've got a groo-vy kind of love._____

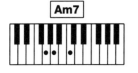
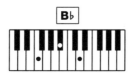
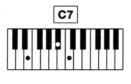
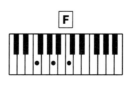
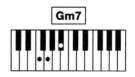

Hotel California

Words and Music by Don Felder, Don Henley and Glenn Frey

Suggested Registration: Marimba
Rhythm: Reggae
Tempo: ♩ = 128

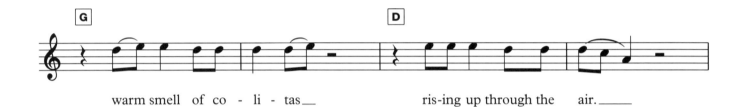

On a dark de-sert high-way,   cold wind in my   hair,

warm smell of co - li - tas__   ris-ing up through the   air. ____

Up a-head in the   dis-tance,   I saw a shim-mer-ing   light,

my head grew hea-vy, and my sight grew dim,   I had to stop for the   night.

There she stood in the   door-way,   I heard the miss - ion   bell,

and I was think-ing   to my-self, this could be hea-ven and this could be   hell. ____

I Love A Lassie

Words and Music by Harry Lauder and Gerald Grafton

Suggested Registration: Clarinet
Rhythm: March
Tempo: ♩ = 112

I love a lass - ie,   a   bon - nie Hie -lan' lass - ie, if ye

saw her you would fan - cy her as   well.   I____   met her in Sep-tem-ber, popped the

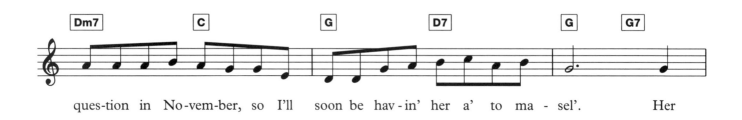

ques - tion in No-vem-ber, so I'll   soon be hav - in' her a' to ma - sel'.   Her

fai - ther has con - sent - ed, so I'm   feel - ing quite con - tent - ed, 'cause I've

been and sealed the bar-gain wi' a kiss. I sit and wea-ry, wea-ry, when I

think a-boot ma dea-ry, an' you'll al-ways hear me sing-ing this:

'I love a lass-ie, a bon-nie bon-nie lass-ie, she's as

pure as the li-ly in the dell. She's as sweet as the hea-ther, the

bon-nie bloom-in' hea-ther, Ma-ry, ma Scotch Blue-bell.'

I'll Be Seeing You

Words by Irving Kahal / Music by Sammy Fain

Suggested Registration: Strings
Rhythm: Swing
Tempo: ♩ = 104

I'll be see-ing you___ in all the old fa-

-mi - liar pla - ces that my heart and mind em-brac-es

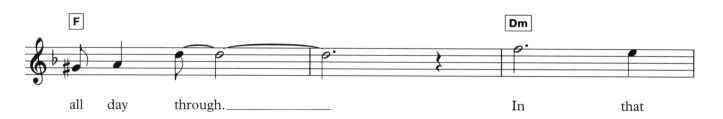

all day through.___ In that

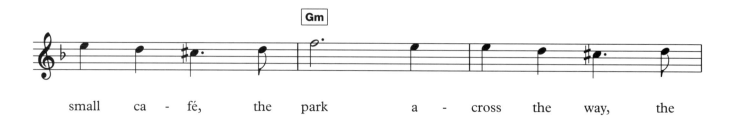

small ca - fé, the park a - cross the way, the

child - ren's ca - rou - sel,___ the chest-nut trees,___ the

wish - ing well.___ I'll be see - ing you___ in

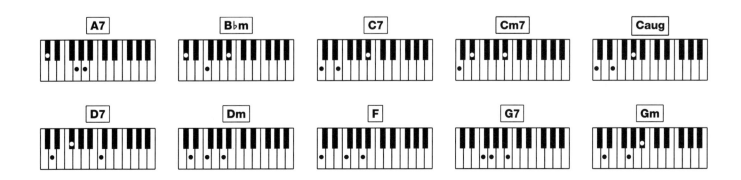

I'M FOREVER BLOWING BUBBLES

Words and Music by Jaan Kenbrovin and John Kellette

Suggested Registration: Muted Trumpet
Rhythm: Waltz
Tempo: ♩ = 140

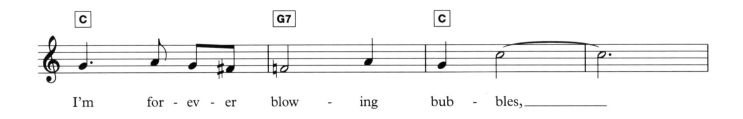

I'm for - ev - er blow - ing bub - bles,_____

pret - ty bub - bles in the air._____

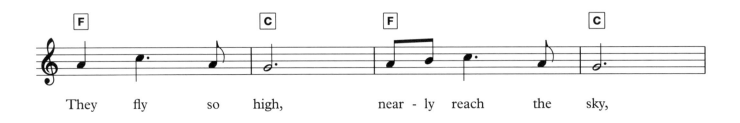

They fly so high, near - ly reach the sky,

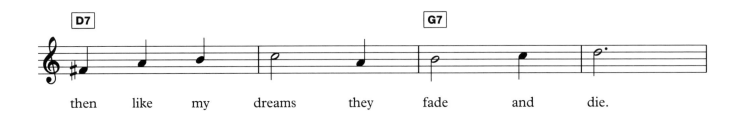

then like my dreams they fade and die.

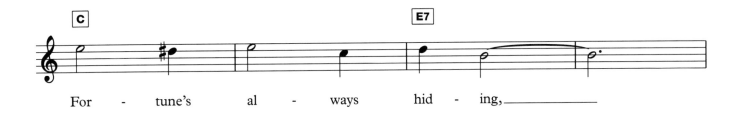

For - tune's al - ways hid - ing,_____

I've looked ev - ery - where._____

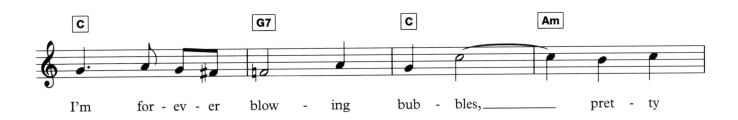

I'm for - ev - er blow - ing bub - bles,_____ pret - ty

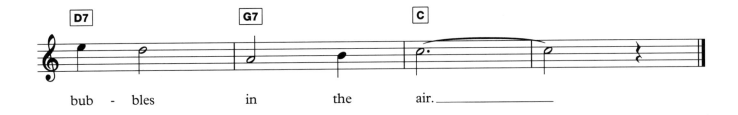

bub - bles in the air._____

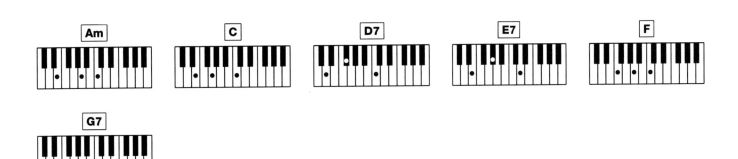

Isn't She Lovely

Words and Music by Stevie Wonder

Suggested Registration: Harmonica
Rhythm: Shuffle
Tempo: ♩ = 112

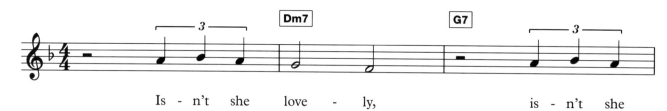

Is - n't she love - ly, is - n't she

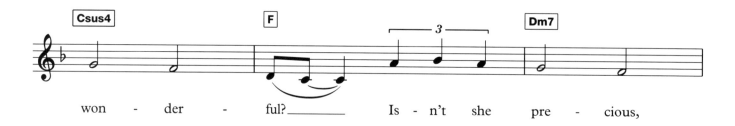

won - der - ful?_____ Is - n't she pre - cious,

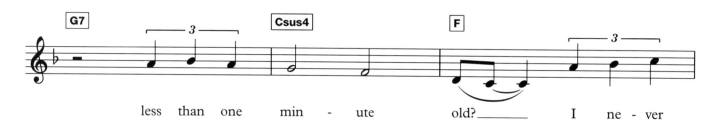

less than one min - ute old?_____ I ne - ver

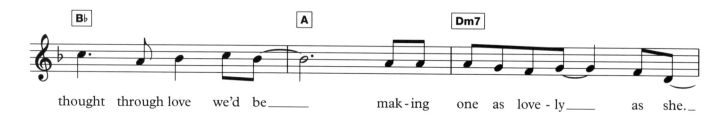

thought through love we'd be_____ mak - ing one as love - ly_____ as she.__

___ Is - n't she love - ly, made from

love?____ Is - n't she pret - ty,

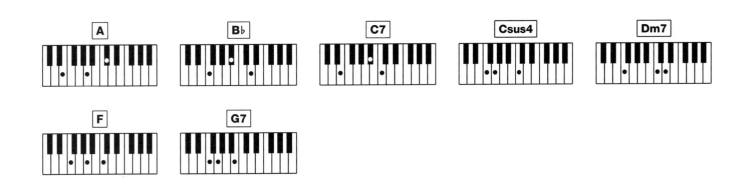

It Had To Be You

Words by Gus Kahn / Music by Isham Jones

Suggested Registration: Jazz Guitar
Rhythm: Medium Swing
Tempo: ♩ = 120

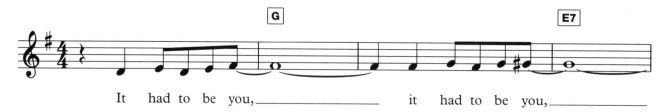

It had to be you,_____ it had to be you,_____

_ I wan-dered a - round,_ and fi-nal-ly found_ the some-bo-dy who_____

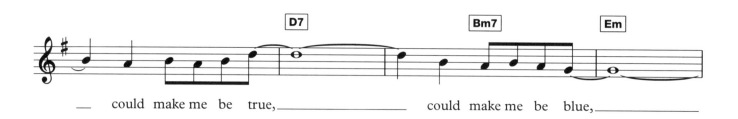

_ could make me be true,_____ could make me be blue,_____

_ and e-ven be glad___ just to be sad,___ think-ing of you._____

_ Some oth-ers I've seen,_____ might ne-ver be mean,_____

might ne-ver be cross,___ or try to be boss,___ but they would-n't do,__

_____ for no-bo-dy else___ gave me a thrill,

__ with all your faults___ I love you still.___ It had to be you,

__ won-der-ful you,___ had to be you._____

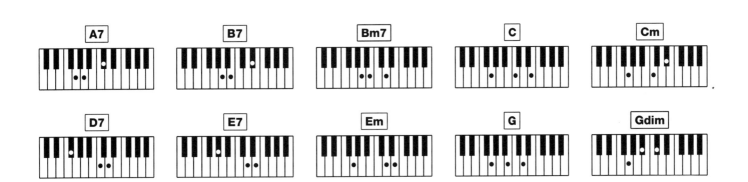

Let's Twist Again

Words and Music by Kal Mann and Dave Appell

Suggested Registration: Saxophone
Rhythm: 8 Beat / Rock 'n' Roll
Tempo: ♩ = 152

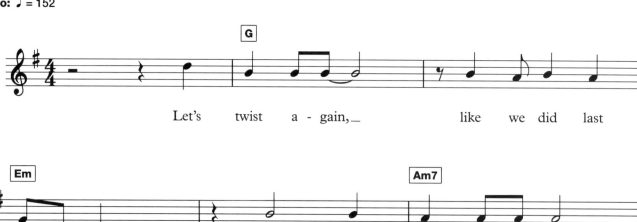

Let's twist a - gain,____ like we did last

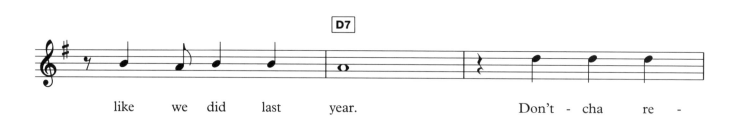

sum - mer,____ yeah, let's twist a - gain,____

like we did last year. Don't - cha re -

- mem - ber when__ things were real - ly hum - min'__

yeah, let's twist a - gain,____ twist - in' time is

here. An' round, an' round an'

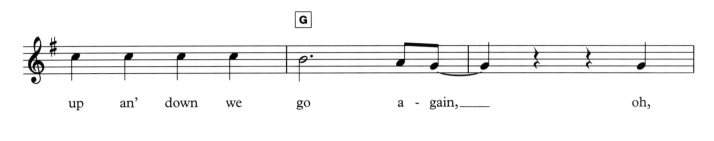

up an' down we go a - gain,____ oh,

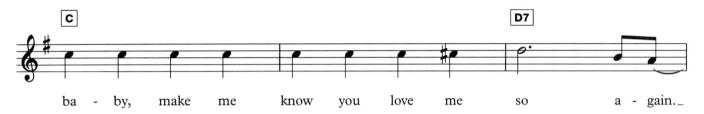

ba - by, make me know you love me so a - gain._

_ Let's twist a - gain,_ like we did last

sum - mer,__ yeah, let's twist a - gain,__

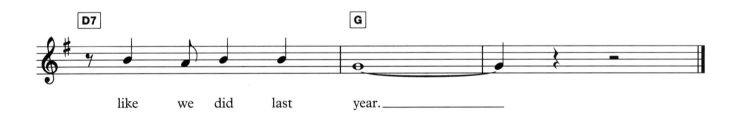

like we did last year._____

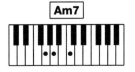

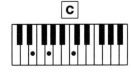

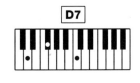

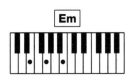

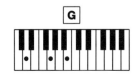

Moonlight Serenade

Words by Mitchell Parish / Music by Glenn Miller

Suggested Registration: Saxophone
Rhythm: Slow Swing
Tempo: ♩ = 72

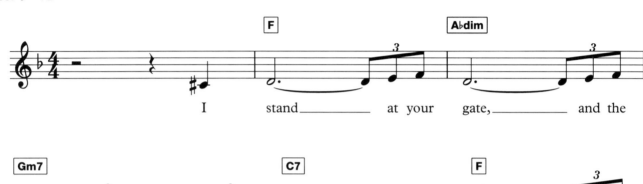

I stand_____ at your gate,_____ and the

song_____ that I sing_____ is of moon - light. I stand_____ and I

wait_____ for the touch___ of your hand___ in the June night. The

ro - ses are sigh - ing a moon - light se - ren -

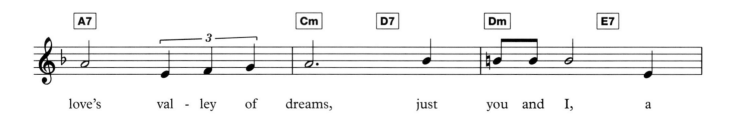

- ade. Let us stray till break of day in

love's val - ley of dreams, just you and I, a

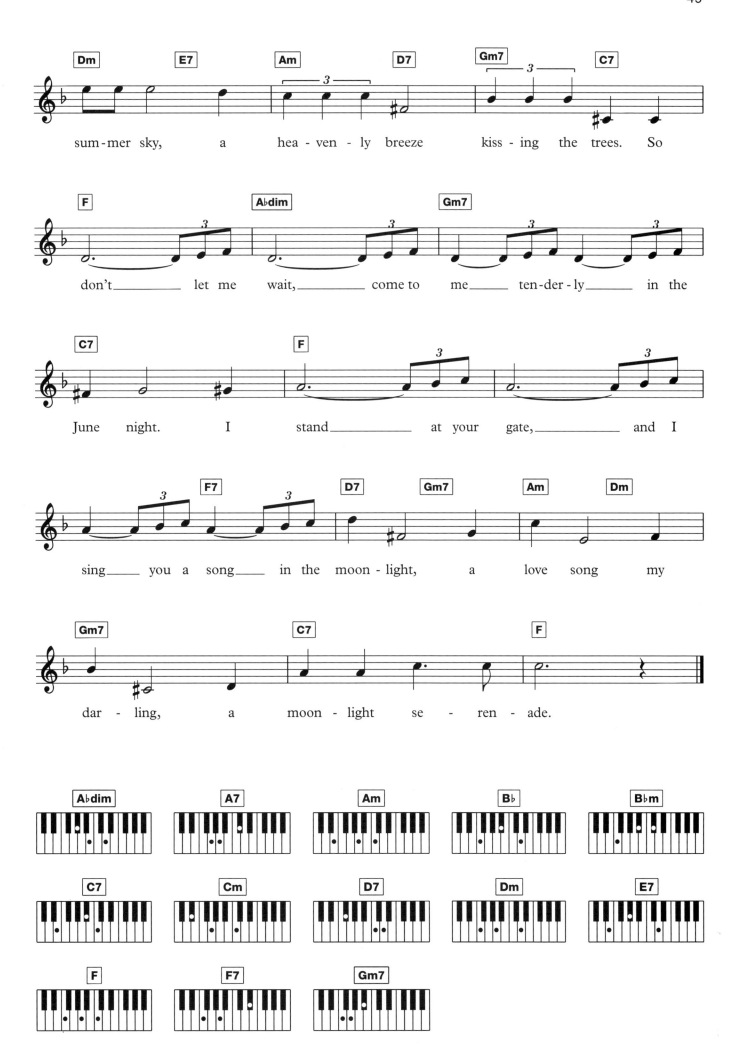

More Than Words

Words and Music by Nuno Bettencourt and Gary Cherone

Suggested Registration: Acoustic Guitar
Rhythm: Soft Rock
Tempo: ♩ = 92

Say-in', 'I___ love___ you' is not the words I want

___ to___ hear___ from you.___ It's not that I___ want___ you

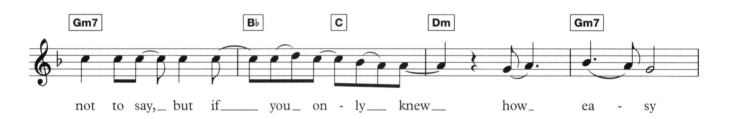

not to say,___ but if___ you___ on - ly___ knew___ how___ ea - sy

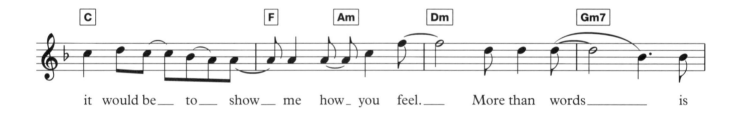

it would be___ to___ show___ me how___ you feel.___ More than words___ is

all you have___ to___ do___ to make it___ real___ then you would-

- n't have___ to say___ that you love___ me,___ 'cause

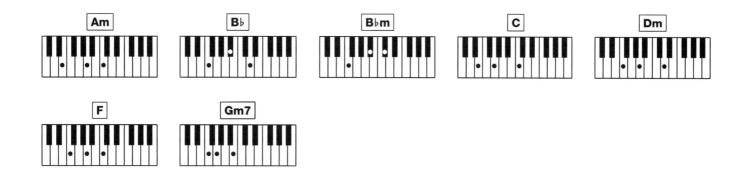

Mustang Sally

Words and Music by Bonny Rice

Suggested Registration: Jazz Organ
Rhythm: Rhythm & Blues
Tempo: ♩ = 120

Mus-tang Sal - ly,

guess you bet-ter slow that Mus-tang down. __

Mus-tang Sal-ly, now ba-by,

guess you bet-ter slow that Mus-tang down. __

You been run-nin' all __ o - ver town, __

I guess you got-ta put your flat feet on the ground.

New York, New York

Words by Fred Ebb / Music by John Kander

Suggested Registration: Piano
Rhythm: Slow Swing
Tempo: ♩ = 106

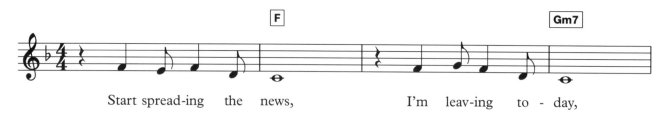

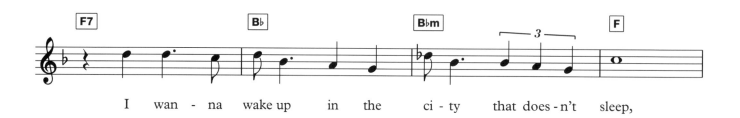

Nikita

Words by Bernie Taupin / Music by Elton John

Suggested Registration: Electric Piano
Rhythm: Soft Rock
Tempo: ♩ = 84

57

Now And Forever

Words and Music by Richard Marx

Suggested Registration: Electric Piano
Rhythm: Soft Rock
Tempo: ♩ = 104

When-ev - er I'm wea-ry___ from the bat-tles that rage in my head,

you make sense of mad - ness, when my sa - ni - ty hangs by a thread.

I lose my way,___ but still___ you seem to un - der -

- stand, now and for - ev - er, I will be___ your_ man.

Now I can rest___ my wor-ries, and al - ways be sure___

that I won't be a - lone___ a - ny - more.   If I'd on - ly   known

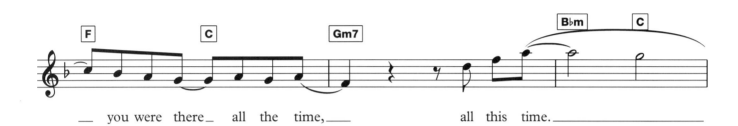

___ you were there_ all the time,___   all this time.___

___ Un - til the day___ the o - cean   does - n't   touch   the___

sand,   now and for-ev - er,   I will be_ your   man.___

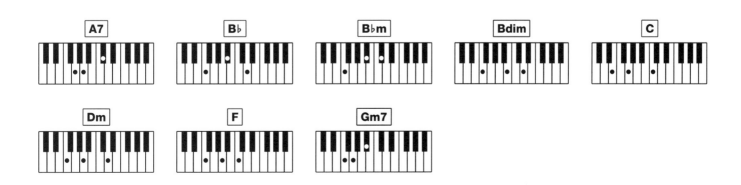

Over The Rainbow

Words by E Y Harburg / Music by Harold Arlen

Suggested Registration: Flute
Rhythm: Soft Rock
Tempo: ♩ = 82

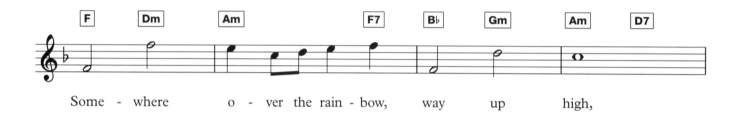

Some - where   o - ver the rain - bow,   way   up   high,

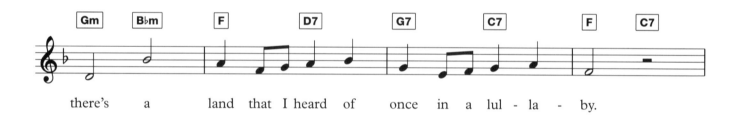

there's   a   land that I heard of   once   in a lul - la - by.

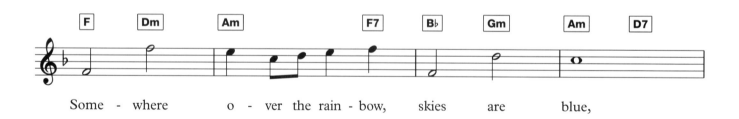

Some - where   o - ver the rain - bow,   skies   are   blue,

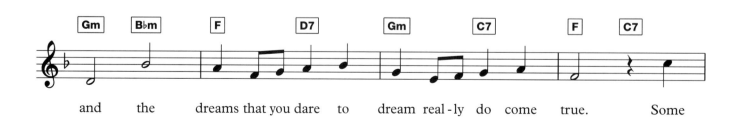

and   the   dreams that you dare   to   dream real - ly do come   true.   Some

day I'll wish up-on a star, and wake up where the clouds are far be-hind me.____

___ Where trou-bles melt like le-mon drops a - way a-bove the chim-ney tops, that's

where you'll find me. Some-where o - ver the rain-bow, blue - birds fly,

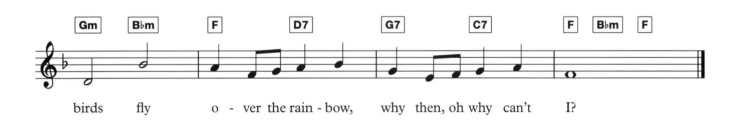

birds fly o - ver the rain - bow, why then, oh why can't I?

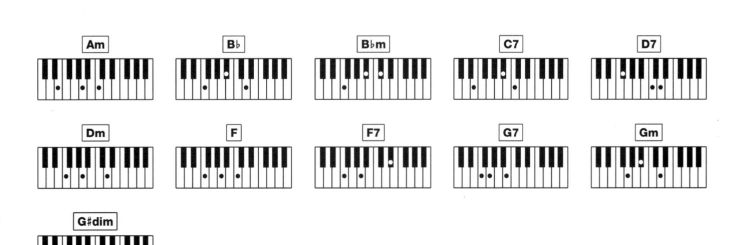

The Pink Panther

By Henry Mancini

Suggested Registration: Tenor Saxophone
Rhythm: Swing
Tempo: ♩ = 98

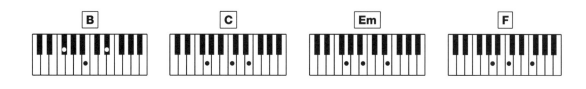

63

Promise Me

Words and Music by Beverley Craven

Suggested Registration: Piano
Rhythm: Soft Rock
Tempo: ♩ = 98

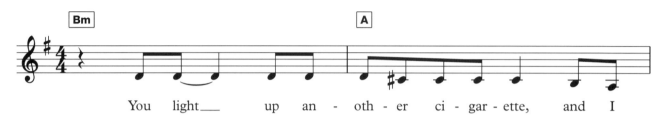

You light___ up an - oth - er ci - gar - ette, and I

pour___ the wine.___ It's four o' - clock in the morn-

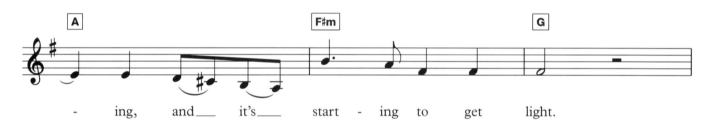

- ing, and___ it's___ start - ing to get light.

When I go a - way___ I'll miss___ you, and I will be think-

- ing of___ you ev - ery night___ and day.___ Just prom - ise me___ you'll

wait for me,___ 'cause I'll be sav - ing all___ my love___ for you,

and I___ will be___ home soon._____

___ Prom - ise me___ you'll wait for me,___ I

need to know you feel___ the same way too,_____

and I'll be___ home, I'll be___ home soon._____

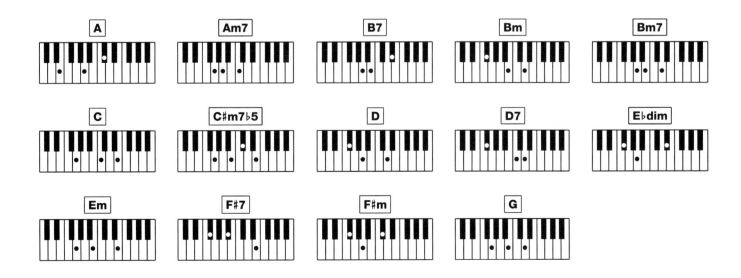

Rudolph The Red-Nosed Reindeer

Words and Music by Johnny Marks

Suggested Registration: Clarinet
Rhythm: Swing
Tempo: ♩ = 132

Ru-dolph the red - nosed rein - deer had a ve - ry shi - ny

nose, and if you ev - er saw it,

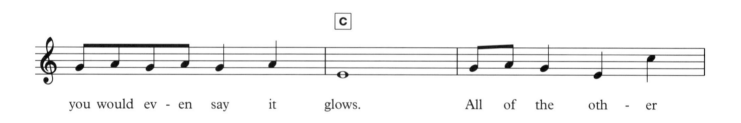

you would ev - en say it glows. All of the oth - er

rein - deer used to laugh and call him names,

they ne - ver let poor Ru - dolph join in a - ny rein - deer games.

The Shadow Of Your Smile

Words by Paul Francis Webster / Music by Johnny Mandel

Suggested Registration: Electric Piano
Rhythm: Beguine
Tempo: ♩ = 96

The sha-dow of your smile when you are

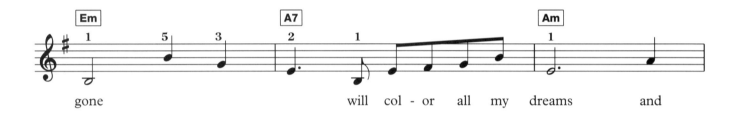

gone will col-or all my dreams and

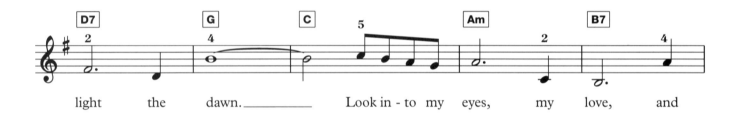

light the dawn._____ Look in-to my eyes, my love, and

see_____ all the love-ly things you are to

me. Our wist-ful lit-tle star was far too

high, a tear-drop kissed your lips and

so did I._____ Now when I re-mem-ber Spring,___

__ all the joy that love can bring,_____ I will be re-mem-ber-ing_____

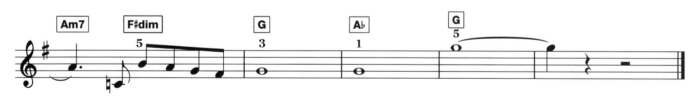

__ the sha-dow of your smile.

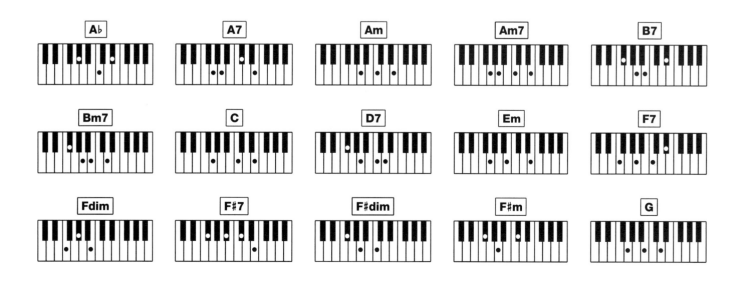

Spread A Little Happiness

Words by Clifford Grey and Greatrex Newman / Music by Vivian Ellis

Suggested Registration: Clarinet
Rhythm: Slow Swing
Tempo: ♩ = 94

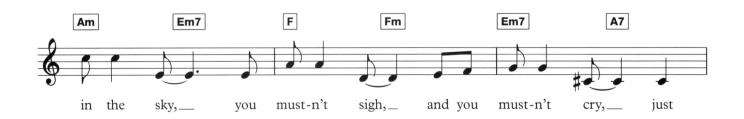

Ev-en when the dark-est clouds are

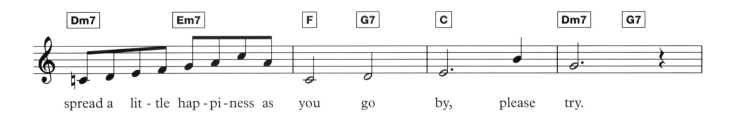

in the sky,__ you must-n't sigh,__ and you must-n't cry,__ just

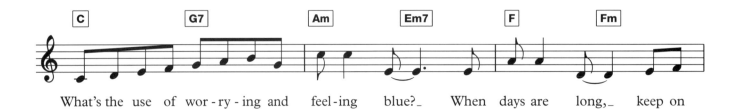

spread a lit-tle hap-pi-ness as you go by, please try.

What's the use of wor-ry-ing and feel-ing blue?_ When days are long,_ keep on

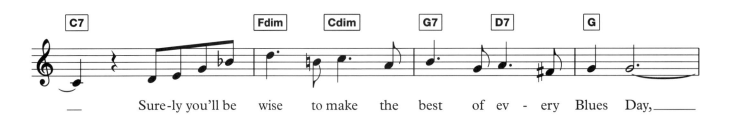

smil-ing through, and spread a lit-tle hap-pi-ness till dreams come true.__

Sure-ly you'll be wise to make the best of ev-ery Blues Day,__

71

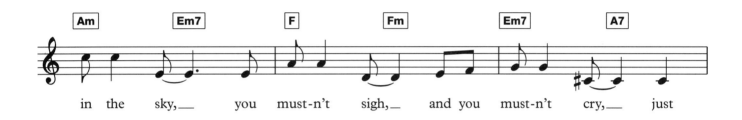

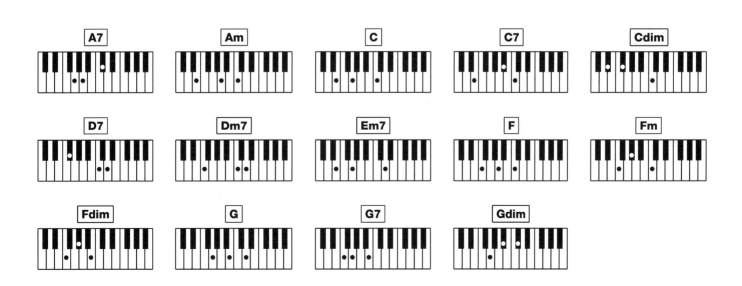

Star Wars (Main Title)

By John Williams

Suggested Registration: Trumpet
Rhythm: March 6/8
Tempo: ♩ = 112

STOP! IN THE NAME OF LOVE

Words and Music by Eddie Holland, Lamont Dozier and Brian Holland

Suggested Registration: Flute
Rhythm: Soul
Tempo: ♩ = 122

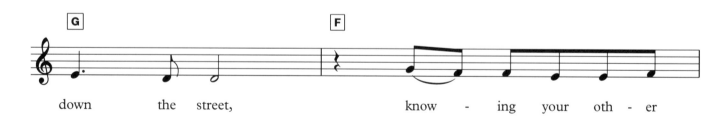

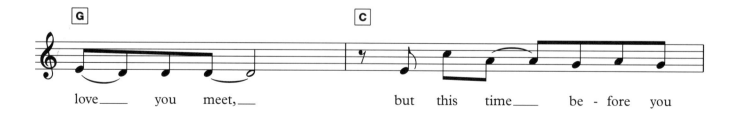

A String Of Pearls

Words by Eddie DeLange / Music by Jerry Gray

Suggested Registration: Tenor Saxophone
Rhythm: Swing
Tempo: ♩ = 116

Ba - by,__ here's__ a five and dime, ba - by,__ now's__ a - bout the time

for a__ string__ of pearls à la Wool - worth.

Ev - ery__ pearl's__ a star a-bove wrapped in__ dreams,__ and filled with love

that old__ string__ of pearls à la Wool - worth.

Till that__ hap - py day in Spring when I__ buy__ the wed-ding ring,

please a__ string__ of pearls à la Wool - worth.

Three Steps To Heaven

Words and Music by Bob Cochran and Eddie Cochran

Suggested Registration: Piano
Rhythm: Slow Latin
Tempo: ♩ = 134

Now there are three_____ steps to

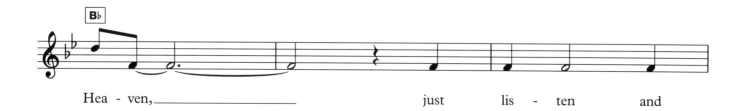

Hea - ven,_____ just lis - ten and

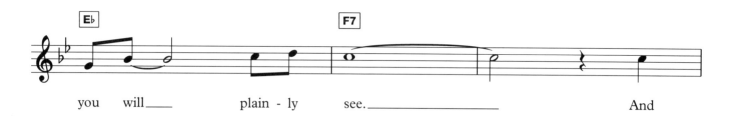

you will____ plain - ly see._____ And

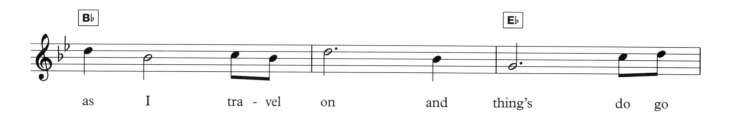

as I tra - vel on and thing's do go

wrong, just call it steps one, two and

three._____ Step one,_____ you

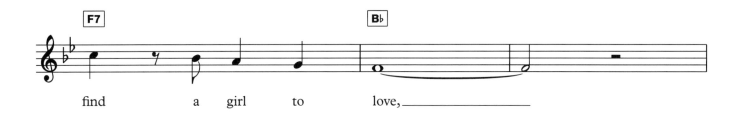

find a girl to love,____

step two,_____ she falls in love with you.____

_ Step three_____ you kiss and hold her

tight - ly,_____ well that sure seems like

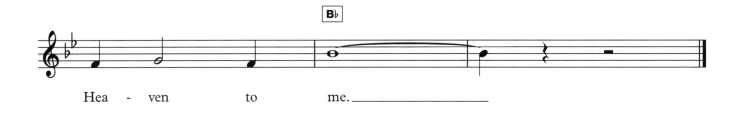

Hea - ven to me._____

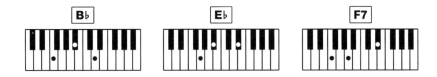

TOOT TOOT TOOTSIE, GOO'BYE

Words and Music by Gus Kahn, Ernest Erdman and Dan Russo

Suggested Registration: Vibraphone
Rhythm: Swing
Tempo: ♩ = 200

Toot toot, Toot - sie, goo' - bye,_____

toot toot, Toot - sie, don't cry._____

The choo - choo train that takes me,

a - way from you, no words can tell how

sad it makes me. Kiss me Toot - sie and

then,_____ do it o - ver a -

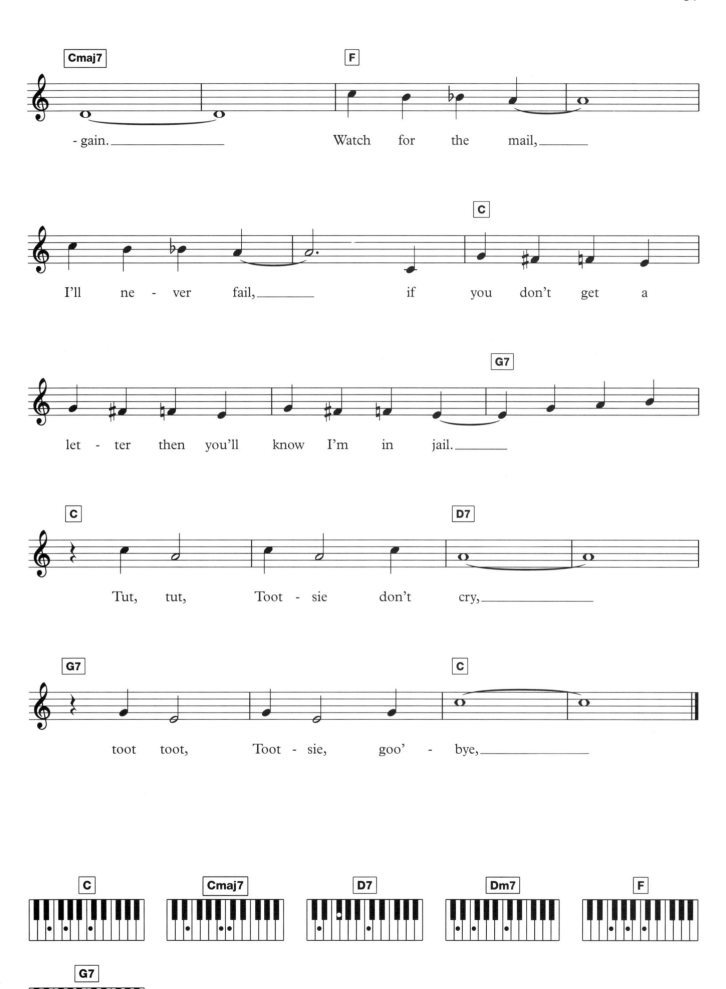

Volare

English Words by Mitchell Parish / Music by Domenico Modugno

Suggested Registration: Accordion
Rhythm: Swing
Tempo: ♩ = 144

Vo - la - re,_____ oh oh,_____ can - ta - re_____

__ oh oh oh oh._____ Let's fly way up to the clouds, a -

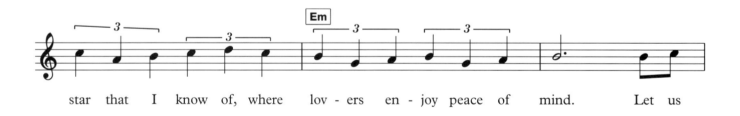

-way from the mad-den-ing crowds. We can sing in the glow of a

star that I know of, where lov-ers en-joy peace of mind. Let us

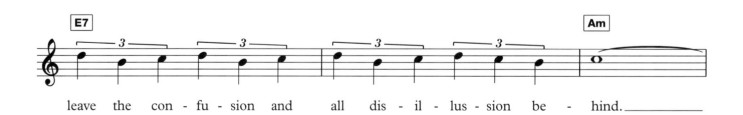

leave the con-fu-sion and all dis-il-lus-sion be - hind._____

Walk On By

Words by Hal David / Music by Burt Bacharach

Suggested Registration: Jazz Organ
Rhythm: Bossa Nova
Tempo: ♩ = 104

If you see me walk-ing down the street, and I start to cry___ each time we meet,

___ walk on by,_____ walk on by.___

___ Make be - lieve___ that you don't see the tears, just

let me grieve in pri-vate, 'cause each time I see you, I break down and

cry. Walk on by._____

I just can't get o - ver los-ing you, and so if I seem___ bro-ken and blue,

walk on by,___ walk on by.___

Fool-ish pride, that's all that I have left, so let me hide___ the

tears, and the sad-ness you gave me when you said good - bye.

Walk on by,_____ don't___ stop, walk on by,___

___ don't stop, walk on by._____

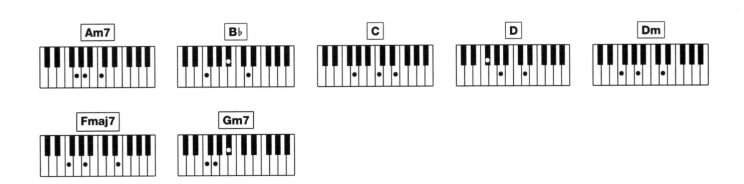

We Have All The Time In The World

Words by Hal David / Music by John Barry

Suggested Registration: Trumpet
Rhythm: Soft Rock
Tempo: ♩ = 96

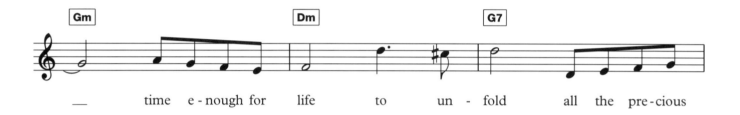

We have all the time in the world,_____

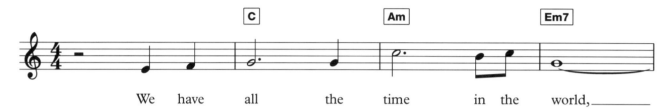

___ time e-nough for life to un-fold all the pre-cious

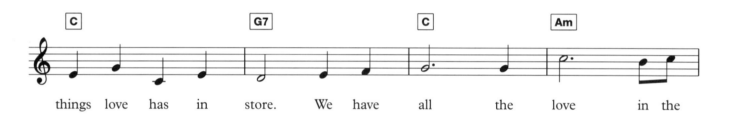

things love has in store. We have all the love in the

world,_____ if that's all we have, you will

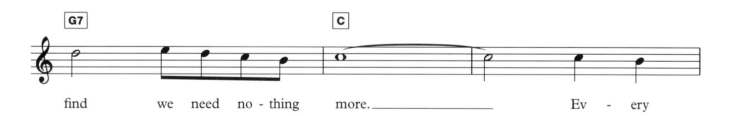

find we need no-thing more._____ Ev-ery

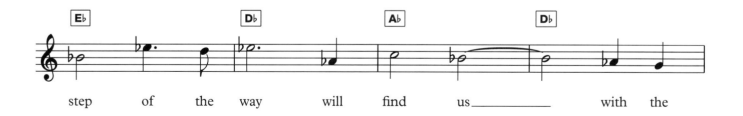

step of the way will find us_____ with the

87

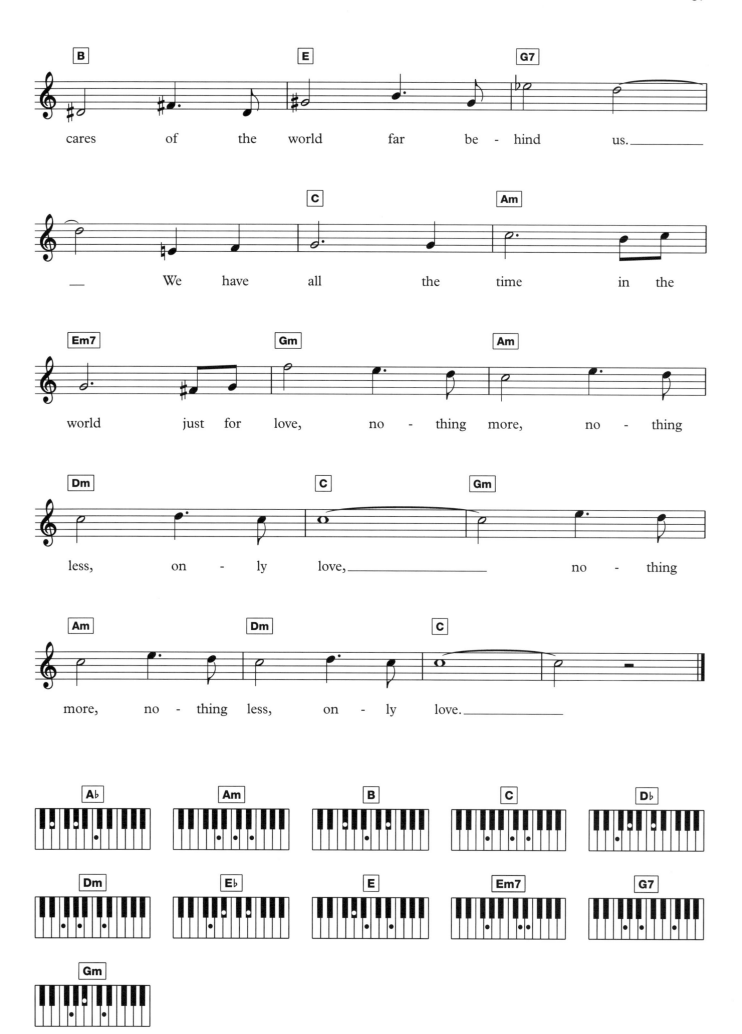

WHAT ARE YOU DOING THE REST OF YOUR LIFE?

Words by Alan and Marilyn Bergman / Music by Michel Legrand

Suggested Registration: Strings
Rhythm: Soft Rock
Tempo: ♩ = 84

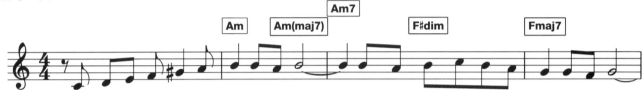

What are you do-ing the rest of your life?___ North and south and east and west of your life?___

___ I have on-ly one re-quest of your life,_____ that you spend it all with me._____

___ All the sea-sons and the times of your days,_____ all the nick-els and the dimes of your days,___

___ let the rea-sons and the rhymes of your days,_____ all be-gin and end with me.

I want to see your face in ev-ery kind of light, in fields of dawn and for-ests of the

89

When A Man Loves A Woman

Words and Music by Calvin Lewis and Andrew Wright

Suggested Registration: Jazz Organ
Rhythm: 6/8 Slow Rock
Tempo: ♩. = 50 (♪ = 150)

When a man___ loves a wo - man,___ can't keep his mind on no-thin' else,_____ he'd change the world for the good thing he's found._____ If she's bad,__ he can't see it,___ she can do no wrong,___ turns his back on his best friend if he put her down. Well this man loves you wo - man,_____ I gave you ev - ery-thing I had,_____

When I Fall In Love

Words by Edward Heyman / Music by Victor Young

Suggested Registration: Vibraphone
Rhythm: Slow Swing / Ballad
Tempo: ♩ = 82

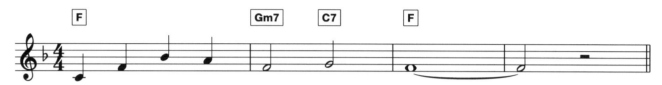

When I fall in love, it will be for - ev - er,

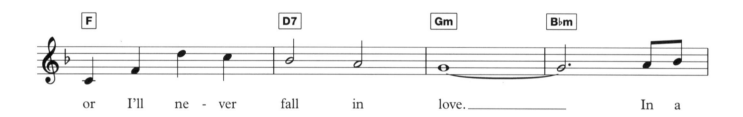

or I'll ne - ver fall in love. _____ In a

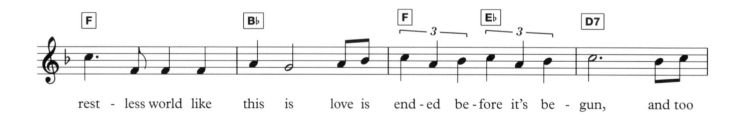

rest - less world like this is love is end - ed be - fore it's be - gun, and too

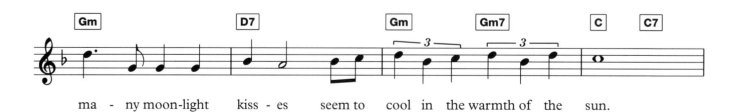

ma - ny moon-light kiss - es seem to cool in the warmth of the sun.

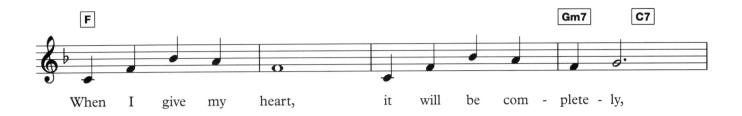

When I give my heart, it will be com - plete - ly,

or I'll ne - ver give my heart._____ And the

mo - ment I can feel that you feel that way too, is

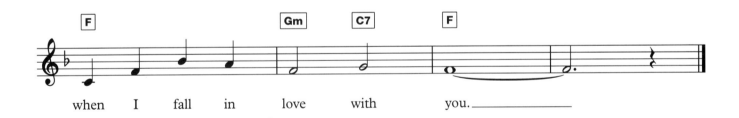

when I fall in love with you._____

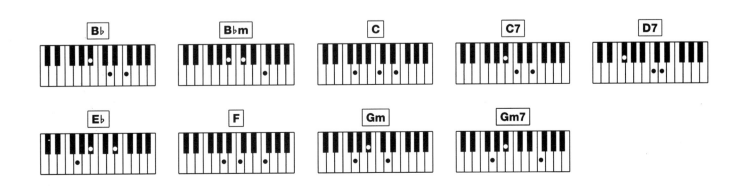

When Irish Eyes Are Smiling

Words by Chauncy Olcott and George Graff / Music by Ernest Ball

Suggested Registration: Accordion
Rhythm: Waltz
Tempo: ♩ = 184

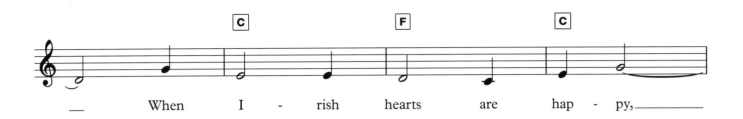

When I - rish hearts are hap - py,____

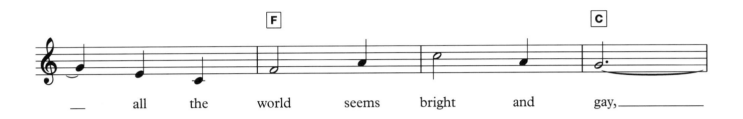

____ all the world seems bright and gay,____

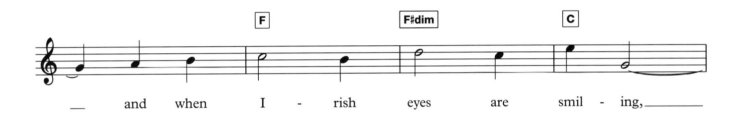

____ and when I - rish eyes are smil - ing,____

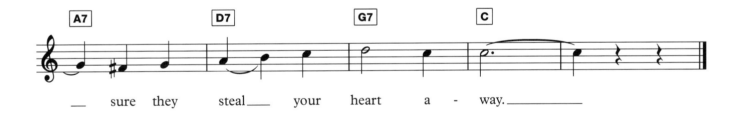

____ sure they steal____ your heart a - way.____

WITHOUT YOU

Words and Music by Pete Ham and Tom Evans

Suggested Registration: Piano
Rhythm: Soft Rock
Tempo: ♩ = 68

Well I can't for-get this eve-ning, or your

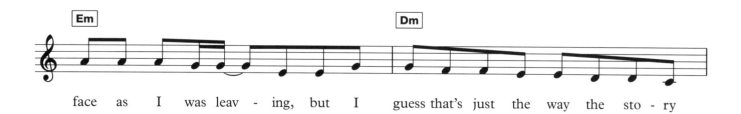

face as I was leav-ing, but I guess that's just the way the sto-ry

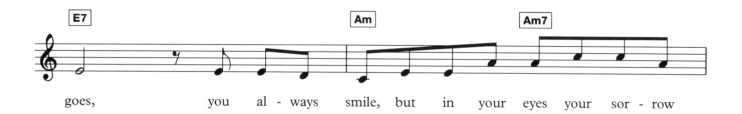

goes, you al-ways smile, but in your eyes your sor-row

shows, yes, it shows. _____ No I

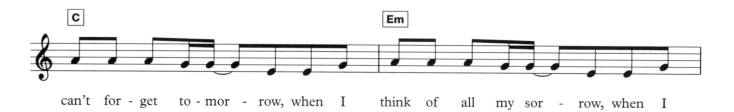

can't for-get to-mor-row, when I think of all my sor-row, when I

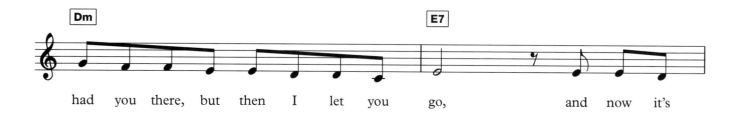

had you there, but then I let you go, and now it's

You've Got A Friend

Words and Music by Carole King

Suggested Registration: Piano
Rhythm: Soft Rock Ballad
Tempo: ♩ = 90

When you're down＿ and trou-bled, and you need＿ some love and care, and no-thing, no-thing is go - ing right, close your eyes,＿ and think of me, ＿ and soon I ＿ will be there, to bright-en up＿ e - ven your dark - est night.

You just call out my name, ＿ and you know wher-ev - er I am, ＿ I'll come run - ning ＿ to see you a - gain.

THE EASY KEYBOARD LIBRARY

Also available in the Decades Series

THE TWENTIES
including:

Ain't Misbehavin'
Ain't She Sweet?
Baby Face
The Man I Love

My Blue Heaven
Side By Side
Spread A Little Happiness
When You're Smiling

THE THIRTIES
including:

All Of Me
A Fine Romance
I Wanna Be Loved By You
I've Got You Under My Skin

The Lady Is A Tramp
Smoke Gets In Your Eyes
Summertime
Walkin' My Baby Back Home

THE FORTIES
including:

Almost Like Being In Love
Don't Get Around Much Any More
How High The Moon
Let There Be Love

Sentimental Journey
Swinging On A Star
Tenderly
You Make Me Feel So Young

THE FIFTIES
including:

All The Way
Cry Me A River
Dream Lover
High Hopes

Magic Moments
Mister Sandman
A Teenager In Love
Whatever Will Be Will Be

THE SIXTIES
including:

Cabaret
Happy Birthday Sweet Sixteen
I'm A Believer
The Loco-motion

My Kind Of Girl
Needles And Pins
There's A Kind Of Hush
Walk On By

THE SEVENTIES
including:

Chanson D'Amour
Hi Ho Silver Lining
I'm Not In Love
Isn't She Lovely

Save Your Kisses For Me
Take Good Care Of My Baby
We've Only Just Begun
You Light Up My Life

THE EIGHTIES
including:

Anything For You
China In Your Hand
Everytime You Go Away
Golden Brown

I Want To Break Free
Karma Chameleon
Nikita
Take My Breath Away

THE NINETIES
including:

Crocodile Shoes
I Swear
A Million Love Songs
The One And Only

Promise Me
Sacrifice
Think Twice
Would I Lie To You?